# A Gu Starting University

By

**Erik Wilson**

# **Content**

2

# **<u>Lecture hacks</u>**

# Introduction

You've finally made it! You're done with school, and you're ready to start being an adult. Over the next few years, you'll make so many new friends, become more independent, and probably drink far too much alcohol. You'll discover how much pasta a person can tolerate, learn that clothes don't magically wash themselves, and more importantly have some of the best and most memorable years of your life!

This guide is designed to provide you with the best advice that any student needs to know before going into their first year of university. It will show you how to have the best social experience that you can possibly have (and how to deal with the hangovers that will undoubtedly come after), give you valuable food and money hacks, and also share the best and most efficient ways to learn lectures and study for your exams.

These are all little university tips and hacks that I and my friends have all adopted over the years, that we all wish that we had been told before that first freshers' week.

# Essentials to bring to Uni that most freshers forget

- Speaker – Although this may not have been a particularly large part of your life before Uni, barely a day will go by in your freshers year when students won't be listening to music on their speaker. It isn't essential that  everyone brings one, but make sure in your house group chat that at least one or two of you do, because chilling in the kitchen, and pre drinks just aren't the same without one.

- Cards – There is no better way to break the ice with your new flatmates, and to get all of them involved in a fun social activity, than to bring cards. Give it two days of Uni, and if you don't already know the rules of Ring of Fire by heart, you will be  sure to by then. Remember cards and liquids don't mix, so don't expect your one pack of cards to last more than a week, so bring a few packs as back-ups.

- Spare bed sheets and towels – A very common mistake for freshers is that they only bring one towel, bed sheet, pillow case and duvet cover. I know, shocking right! That your bed sheets and towels won't magically change themselves anymore, but after 1 month of sleeping in the same sheets, you will be very grateful for this tip.

- Tupperware boxes – You will soon learn that cooking a big batch of food at once, and then simply reheating it later on will save you so much time and effort. I didn't get round to buying a Tupperware box for at least 3 months, and was constantly annoying my flatmates by borrowing theirs, so don't make the same mistakes I did.

- Electric fan – You may not think that a fan is a necessity, but many of the university halls can get unbearably hot, even in September when you move in. Also, having 6 + people crammed into your small kitchen really can increase the temperature, so you will instantly become a flat favourite if you've got a fan that can help everyone out.

- Sports equipment – If you play a sport that requires equipment, then definitely don't hesitate to bring it with you, even if you're not sure if you want to play that sport at uni.

- Plastic cups, shot glasses and ping pong balls – Plastic cups are always an essential for any pre drinks, and as many nights progress shot glasses often get brought out. Beer pong is the most classic drinking game, and it is almost guaranteed that your fellow flatmates will have forgotten to bring ping pong balls.

- Laptop – Having your own laptop is, sadly, an essential for university. Your library will provide some computers, but these will often all be taken, so you will really need your  own laptop when it comes to exam time. It is also very useful for watching Netflix, because many first year halls don't have a TV.

- Shit shirt – You are almost guaranteed to have a shit shirt social very early into your uni life, so why waste money buying one there when you can just bring one from home? If  you don't have one yourself, then your dad or other older male member of your family will be sure to have one of their 'normal' shirts that they can 'lend' you. But, do not expect to give it back to them in a wearable condition, and maybe refrain from saying that you only need it for a shit shirt social. Or you can always get one from a charity shop.

# Social life

There is a reason why social life is the first category to come up in this book, and that is because, as a fresher, this is what university is all about. You may or may not have heard, but for nearly all courses your first year doesn't count towards your degree! Sadly this isn't the case for your second and third year of university (and the work becomes much harder), so this means that when you're a fresher you really have to make the most of the crazy and fantastic social experience that university has to offer! Many people make the mistake of working a little too hard at the start of first year, and not making the most of all of the social life that university has to offer. This is exactly the time to let yourself go a bit crazy, before calming down and focussing more on your studies in your later years.

This chapter will tell you the do's and don'ts that will help you to have the best social experience possible at uni.

# Fresher's wristband

To buy or not to buy a fresher's wristband will be a guaranteed question that will pop up in your house group chat before going to uni. It is often very unclear what events these wristbands get you into, and there are often multiple wrist bands available to buy. Buying a wristband ties you down to going to exactly those events and no other ones, and if you buy different wristbands to your flatmates, then you will not be able to go to the same events. The freshers' event websites will often say that the events are nearly sold out, and yet you will turn up to the events and still be able to buy tickets (sometimes even cheaper than online) at the door.

From past experience I would definitely say that it is **not** worth splashing out on a wristband and recommending that your flatmates also don't. Instead, perhaps just buy tickets to one of two of the main events.

# Socialise as much as possible

This is especially important during freshers' week! Go and make friends with your neighbouring flats, invite them to hang out or for pre drinks. The more people you get to know right at the start, the better chance you have of making some good and solid friendships very early on. Remember everyone else is in the same boat as you and won't know many, if any, people, so they will be more than happy to hang out with you. This also gives you a chance to meet some people who do the same course as you, so you won't be walking to that dreaded first lecture on your own.

After a few days of freshers' week, you may be feeling unbelievably tired and hungover, but it really is worth powering through, and meeting as many new people as possible. Who knows, they might be one of your best friends just a few months' later. A quick warning though, you will get very bored of introducing yourself hundreds of times, but this phase won't last long.

# **Keeping the peace with your flat**

It is very important to stay on good terms with your flatmates. A year can be a very long time if there is a falling out and some awkwardness amongst your flatmates. Relationships amongst flatmates may seem like a good idea at the time, but they often end badly, and this is one of the main causes of rifts.

Although they can work out on occasions, every uni student will know of at least one first year house that was made awkward due to flatmates sleeping together.

You have to decide who you are living with for your second year in about January of your first year, which means that you are very likely to end up living with at least a few of your housemates. This is even more reason to remain friends the whole way through, and to do everything that you can to keep it this way.

# Societies

If you take one thing away from this book, then it should be that joining a society will have a great a positive impact on your university experience. Societies range from sports societies, to bridge society, to drama societies, and we even had a 'meal deal society' at my university! You do not need to have any experience in the society that you'd like to join, and it is a great chance to meet new people, and to learn a new skill. All societies are very welcoming, and they always love to get new members coming in (regardless if you've never even heard of what the society is about before).

Just remember to respect your senior society members, because unlike at school you are now at the bottom of the food chain again. Don't worry, your time will come in later years when you will then be able to order the freshers around.

If you would like to find out more about what societies exist, what the people are like, and how to join them, then all you need to do is go down to freshers' fair. This is usually held just after freshers' week, and your student union will be sure to let you know when and where it is. Representatives of all societies will be there, and they will be more than willing to answer any of your questions and will definitely be trying to persuade you that their society is the one for you. If this has not been enough to win you over, then freshers' fair is the number one place for free food. You will be guaranteed free pizza, ice cream and many more tasty snacks.

# **Sports night**

Whether you are an avid athlete, or have no interest in sport whatsoever, sports night is an absolute essential night out, and is almost guaranteed to be the biggest night out your uni has to offer every week. All sports matches are played on a Wednesday, and to celebrate their victories or drown their sorrows, every uni around the country has a big night out (usually in their SU) afterwards. You just have to hope that your timetable is kind to you and doesn't give you the dreaded 9am start on a Thursday. If that is the case your lecturers will often cut you some slack. They understand what a Thursday morning means.

If you join a society that is not sports related, then it is also university tradition to attend sports night, and go with your fellow society members, which means that no one misses out.

Sports night is the one night of the week where nightclubs don't care what you wear or what state you are in for that matter. On an average sports night there will be people in togas, many pub golfers, and even sometimes students dressed up as babies. Over the course of the year you will be sure to see more types of fancy dress than you ever thought imaginable.

# **Initiations**

It is indeed true that most societies will require freshers to be initiated, but don't worry, most of them really aren't too bad. Everyone there has been initiated themselves, and at the end of the day it is all about having fun. It is true that you will probably end up drinking more than you've ever drunk before, but the seniors will do this in a fun way that will involve lots of games and getting to know each other. It is safe to say, though, that if you have not thrown up at uni before this point, then this will almost certainly be changing right then. If initiations are not for you then that is absolutely fine as well! Just simply speak to the social sec of your society, and they will always understand if you don't want to do them.

Do be warned however, a few of the sports initiations can be a level or two past fun. Rugby is renowned for having pretty brutal initiations, and hockey is also meant to be tough.

# **Fancy dress**

If you do decide to join a society, then you will be guaranteed to have many fancy-dress-themed Wednesday nights. Some examples of fancy dresses that I have had to do myself for socials at university include Toga social, generation social (freshers wear baby clothes, second years wear school clothes, third years are grandparents, and anyone older is a skeleton), charity shop social (all clothes worn must be from a charity shop), pairs or pears (have a matching outfit as someone or dress as a pear), dress as an animal that starts with the same letter as your name, and there are many more. House parties are nearly always themed as well, so don't just be expecting to be dressing up on a Wednesday night.

The Toga social is one that is a must for every society, so it seems fitting that you get a guide showing you how to actually make a toga.

1. Buy a double (if you are very small you may get away with a single) white bedsheet without the elastic fitted edges if possible.

2. Grab the corner of the sheet in one hand. Leave about 20cm past your hand to tie the knot with. Hold the bed sheet above either shoulder.

3. Drape the bed sheet snug across your chest, and then tuck it under the opposite arm.

4. If the toga is too long, then fold over one edge and try again until it is about knee height.

5. Wrap the toga around your back. Tuck the sheet under the arm that you're already holding it with, and then once more around the front of your chest, under the opposite arm, and across your back.

6. Tie the toga. Bring the second corner of the toga up over your back to the corner in your hand. Then either tie a knot to fasten it or use a safety pin or brooch if you have them.

Just like that you're ready to head to the party/social and show off your perfectly made toga.

# **Pre drinking games**

You may think that people going to uni will already be big drinkers, but that is often not the case. Many students going into freshers will have only recently turned 18 and won't have had much experience with alcohol and nights out. Knowing a few good pre-drinking games is the perfect way to seem like you're a veteran of the game, and is a great way to get to know your flatmates and newly found friends a little better.

Ring of fire:

This is your basic university drinking game that is essential to know during freshers, but I can promise you that by second year you will have grown bored of it, and moved onto new games.

You lay the cards face down in a circle around the cup in the middle, ensuring that there are no gaps between the cards. You take it in turns picking up one of the cards around the table, and each card has a different action.

Ace: waterfall, everyone in turn around the table starts drinking, and you can only stop when the person to your left does unless you finish your drink.

2 – You: nominate someone to drink.

3 – Me: You drink.

4 – Any girls at the table drink.

5 – Thumb master: whoever gets a 5 can put their thumb on the table, and then the last person in the room to do so drinks.

6 – Any boys at the table drink.

7 – Heaven: whoever gets the 7 can point up to the sky, and then the last person to do so drinks.

8 – Mate: pick someone to drink anytime you drink for the rest of the game.

9 – Rhyme: say any word, and then go left around the table with words that rhyme with it until someone can't think of one. They then drink.

10 – Categories: pick a category (like 'cities in the UK?'), go left around the room until someone cannot think of an answer. They then drink.

Jack: Make up a rule

Queen: You become question master. Ask people questions and if they reply, then they have to drink, but if they say fu*k you question master, then you have to drink.

King: Add some of your drink to the cup in the middle.

When the circle gets broken meaning there is a gap between the cards in the circle, then the person who created that gap has to drink. The game finishes when someone turns over the fourth king, and they then have to down the nasty concoction of drinks that there is in the middle cup.

# **Ride the bus**

There are multiple versions of this game, and the rules seem to differ across the whole country. These rules consist of many adaptations of different people's versions that I consider to be the best.

1. Deal each player four cards and have them place them in front of themselves face down WITHOUT looking at their cards.

2. Deal eight cards into the middle of the table, making it two rows of four cards that are face down.

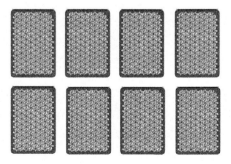

3. The first person then guesses whether their card on the left is red or black. If they get it right,

then they give out one sip, but if they get it wrong then they drink one sip themselves. Everyone at the table then does this.

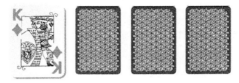

So, in this case if you said red then give out one sip, and if not drink one.

4. Then the first person guesses whether their next card will be higher or lower than the previous one. If they get it right then they give out two sips, but if they get it wrong then they drink two sips themselves. Repeat around the table

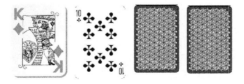

So, in this case if you said lower (which you should always say on a king) then give out 2 sips, and if not drink twice.

5. The third card is outside or in between. Before looking at the card choose whether it will be outside, or in between your two previous cards.

E.g.: if your two last cards are a seven and a jack, then eight would be in between, and king would be outside. Get it right and give out three sips, but get it wrong and drink three yourself.

So, in this case if you had said in between the king and the ten give out three sips, and if not drink three sips.

6. The fourth card is choosing the suit. The odds of getting this one right are slightly tougher, so get this right and you give out six sips, but get it wrong and you only drink two sips.

So, in this case if you had said diamonds give out 6 sips, but if you guessed any of the other suits, then drink 2 sips.

7. Now everyone's four cards should be face up in front of them, with the eight cards face down in the middle. Choose one row of the eight cards (so one of the rows of four) to be the 'dish out drinks' row, and the other row to be the 'consume yourself' row.

8. Turn over the first card from the consume row, and whoever has that cards value drinks once. Then turn over the second card from that row and whoever has that drinks twice … until all four cards are turned over from that row.

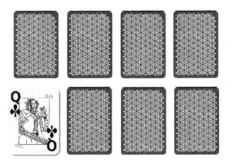

So, in this case anyone who has a queen must drink one sip.

9. Then turn over the first card of the second row, and whoever has that card gives out one sip to a person of their choice. Turn over the second card, and whoever has that gives out two sips to a person of their choice …

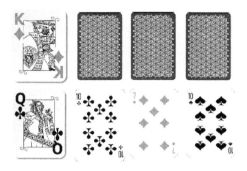

So, in this case anyone that has a king gives out one sip.

This game is a personal favourite of mine, but beware, a lot of alcohol will be drunk over the course of it, so don't play it if you've already drunk a lot.

# **Drinking games to play without cards**

Categories:

One person picks a category, and it must be a category that has quite a few answers (e.g. different types of dog breeds). Then go around one at a time in the room saying an answer to the category until there is only one person left. To make this a drinking game then you can say the loser drinks X times where X is the number of people in the room (so say five people are playing, the loser drinks five times), the second last drinks X-1 times (so 5 people playing, they drink 4 times) and so on, so that the winner drinks one sip.

Ping pang pong:

This is a game that you need at least four people to play. Someone proposes a game of ping pang pong either to their left or right. Say you propose the game to your left, then you say ping, the person to your left says pang, and the person to their left says pong. Then the person who they make eye contact with says ping, and the cycle starts again. This game may sound easy, but after a few drinks it can get very confusing!

Never have I ever:

This is a classic drinking game that you're almost certain to have heard of. Go round in a circle and everyone says never have I ever done something. Then if you've done the thing that they're saying then you have to drink. This is a great way to get to know your new flatmates and friends, and maybe even find out a little too much about them.

Most likely to:

You go around the room and say "most likely to" followed by a hypothetical question. E.g. most likely to text their ex tonight. Then everyone chooses someone to point at who they think is most likely to do this, and that person has to drink. This game can get a little personal, so make sure you know the people well who you are playing it with.

# **Chants**

Every university has their own unique chants, but there are some universal chants that you will likely hear at pres all around the country, so why not impress your new friends by knowing the chants off by heart already. In classic university style they mostly revolve around finishing your drink.

1.

We like to drink with X because X is our mate, and when we drink with X he/she gets it down in 8..7..6..5..4..3..2..1

2.

| One person: | Rest of the group: |
|---|---|
| Where is he/shefrom? | Finland |
| And what does he/she speak? | |

All together:

Finish…Finish…Finish…Finish

# **Hangovers and hangover cures**

It seems only fitting that the section to follow pre-drinking games would be how to cure the hangovers that they will undoubtedly give you. Feeling sorry for yourself and hungover in bed is sadly a very common occurrence for many students in first year, but there are many little tips and tricks to ease the pounding on your head.

VKs:

Some of you reading this may have never heard of a VK, but when you go to uni this is almost certain to change. A VK is a little 330ml bottle of 4% alcoholic fruit juice effectively, and although they may taste very nice whilst drunk on your night out, I can promise you that drinking too many will make your hangover twice as bad the day after. I definitely wouldn't say stay away from them, but if you don't want to have a pounding headache the day after, then don't drink more than two or three in a night.

Drinking water:

Regardless of what state you return home in, drinking a pint of water before going to bed does a world of good for your hangover the day after. One drink roughly equates to your body losing about 100ml of water, which means that if you have 10 drinks over the course of a night, then your body has lost about one litre of water meaning you will become dehydrated. If you don't drink water before going to sleep, then you will be far more likely to wake up with a headache, simply because you will be very dehydrated.

Shower:

Having a shower the morning after is also a great way of reviving yourself from your hangover, and getting ready to be productive during the day.

Dark coloured drinks:

Do not drink dark coloured drinks if you would like to stay hangover free. They contain natural chemicals called congeners, which irritate blood vessels and tissue in the brain and can make a hangover worse. Many freshers make the mistake of drinking too much red wine, and then severely paying for the consequences the day after.

Don't drink on an empty stomach:

This isn't necessarily a hangover cure, but just a good general rule of drinking. Having food in your stomach (carbs are the best e.g. pasta) soaks up some of the alcohol, which will stop you from getting too drunk too fast. It really does make a massive difference if you go on a night out without having dinner, and this is when people often get themselves in states beyond enjoyment. You may hear the phrase 'eating is cheating', but don't let this peer pressure you into not having your dinner!

# **Food**

Food is an area where students come in at very different levels and abilities. My flat ranged from someone who had never so much as cooked a pizza (and the first time they cooked pasta, they tried putting it in the kettle and turning the kettle on), to someone who was constantly baking and making very advanced dishes. You do not have to end uni as a brilliant cook, but it is vital that you learn the basics early on. This section will teach you cooking tips that I wish I had been told earlier, and five easy to follow dishes that every student should know.

## **Meal sharing**

Surprisingly at uni, not that many people actually decide to cook meals together. There are so many reasons why cooking together will make your cooking experience so much more enjoyable:

1. Cooking on your own can get a little boring, so meal sharing ensures that you always cook with one of your friends.
2. You only have to cook every other day! It saves so much time and effort!

**3.** It motivates you to cook tastier, more adventurous, and healthier meals. You can't let your cooking buddy down with a bad meal.

I only started doing meal sharing in my second year of uni and it really transformed my cooking. I was no longer making pasta six days a week, but instead started cooking many new dishes that I would never have bothered to do if I were just cooking for myself.

# <u>Cooking in bulk</u>

Cooking in bulk is another excellent way to save time cooking. You will struggle to find any student who hasn't cooked a big batch of Bolognese, and then put it the fridge or freezer so that it can simply be reheated later on in the week. A Tupperware box with a lid is essential for this, because if you just leave your food in a bowl in the fridge it can become very dry and lose its taste. Bulk cooking pasta or rice can also be time-saving, but I find that if left for more than a day or two they can start to become stale.

# Doing big shops vs lots of little shops

Over time you will quickly learn that doing big shops is by far the better option than only shopping for each individual meal. Often freshers do the latter, but there are numerous reasons why this is not as good:

1. Doing big shops at a superstore saves you money. Buying the big bag of rice, or the big box of chicken is always cheaper than buying the smaller versions. Also buying from smaller shops tends to be more expensive than their superstore counterparts. Just be careful not to buy so much that your food starts going out of date!
2. It saves you time as you are not constantly going to the shops.
3. It is easier to set a food budget if you aren't making as many trips to the shop.
4. Online food shopping is a thing!! For the meagre price of about £2.50 they will deliver all of your food to your door.

# What cooking gear to bring

- Wok

- Frying pan

- Cooking pot

- Cheese grater

- Chopping board

- Sharp knife

- Pasta bake dish

- Baking tray

- Colander

It isn't essential that you bring all of these items, but it is important that there is at least one of each in your kitchen.

# Five easy recipes that every student must master

## Bolognese

This is the most common student meal that absolutely everyone needs to know! There are variations to the ingredients, but this is my trusted recipe.

Ingredients:

2 tablespoons of olive oil

400g beef mince (or can substitute mushrooms or peppers for vegetarians)

1 onion, diced

2 garlic cloves, chopped

2 tins of chopped tomatoes

Squeeze of tomato puree

400ml of oz stock (ideally beef but others are also okay)

400g of dried spaghetti

Salt and pepper

Optional: teaspoon of dried herbs

Grated cheese

Method:

1. Heat a large saucepan over medium heat. Add a tablespoon of olive oil to the pan before putting your mince in. Spread the mince out and add a pinch of salt and pepper. Cook until the mince is a brown colour all over. Once browned, transfer the mince to a bowl set aside.

2. At the same time you start cooking the mince, heat a large saucepan of water and add a pinch of salt. Once the water is boiling place the spaghetti in. Spaghetti takes about 8-12 minutes to cook depending on how you like it. Once it is cooked drain the water and leave the spaghetti in the colander.

3. Add another tablespoon of oil to the saucepan you cooked the mince in and turn the heat to medium. Add the onions and a pinch of salt and cook for about 5 minutes. Then add the garlic and cook for a further 2 minutes. After this add your cooked mince back into the pan and stir it all together.

**4.** Add the tomatoes to the pan and stir it well. Pour in the stock and reduce to a simmer. This next step depends on how much time you have. Ideally this sauce should be left to simmer for 45 minutes, but if you do not have much time, then you can do it in less.

**5.** Add the pasta to the Bolognese sauce and mix it together well. Add grated cheese at this point if you want any.

# __Fajitas__

Ingredients:

2 teaspoons of olive oil

450g of boneless chicken breast (or use a can of chili beans as a vegetarian option)

Salt and pepper

2 bell peppers, de-seeded and sliced into small pieces

2 onions, diced

Wraps

Smokey bbq seasoning (or others of your choice)

Guacamole

Salsa

Soured cream

Grated cheese


Fajitas have quite a few ingredients, but the process of cooking them is very easy.

Method:

**1.** Cut your chicken breasts into bite sized cubes.

**2.** Get a large pan and put 1 tablespoon of oil in the pan over a medium heat. Add your diced chicken and cook until golden and cooked through. To test this, cut open a few pieces of your chicken, and if they are white all of the way through then they are cooked. Just before they are cooked through, add half of your smokey bbq seasoning and stir the chicken. Once cooked, remove the chicken from the pan and place in a bowl.

**3.** Put another tablespoon of oil into your pan and keep it on medium heat. Then add your sliced bell peppers, and diced onion to the pan and cook until soft or for 5 minutes. Add the chicken and mix it all together.

**4.** Serve with your wraps, add guacamole, salsa soured cream and cheese and enjoy!

# Pasta bake

Ingredients:

1 tablespoon of olive oil

1 onion, chopped

1 garlic clove, chopped

Pasta bake sauce

150g of pasta

50g of cheddar, grated

2 chicken breasts, diced


Method:

Pre-heat the oven to 200 degrees C

1. Heat 1 tablespoon of oil in a medium sized pan and add the diced chicken, with a pinch of salt and pepper. Cook the chicken until golden brown on each side and cooked through. When cooked, place the chicken in a bowl to the side.

2. Meanwhile cook the pasta according to the pack instructions.

3. After the chicken has been cooked, heat another tablespoon of oil in the medium pan, and fry the

onion for 5 minutes until softened and slightly golden. Add in the garlic and cook for a further 2 minutes.

**4.** Drain the pasta and place into your pasta bake dish. Add the chicken, onion, garlic, and pasta bake sauce and mix it all together. Grate your cheese onto the pasta mixture.

**5.** Place the pasta bake into the oven for 15 minutes at 200 degrees C, and your pasta bake is done.

# **Chicken stir-fry**

Ingredients:

2 tablespoons of olive oil (or sunflower oil)

Fresh/frozen vegetable stir-fry mix

1.5 chicken breasts, diced (or use cashew nuts or tofu as a vegetarian option)

150g of basmati rice

2 tablespoons of soy sauce

Salt and pepper

1 garlic clove, crushed

Method:

1. Heat 1 tablespoon of oil in a medium sized wok and add the diced chicken, with a pinch of salt and pepper. Cook the chicken until golden brown on each side and cooked through. When cooked place the chicken in a bowl to the side.

2. Meanwhile boil about 300ml of water in a pot and add a cup and a bit of rice. Cook for 16-18 minutes.

**3.** Once the chicken is cooked, heat 1 tablespoon of oil in your wok on high heat and add your stir-fry mixture. Cook for 5 minutes, or until all of the vegetables are cooked but not too soft. Just before it is done add some soy sauce, and a splash of water.

**4.** Drain the rice, then add the stir-fry and chicken to your rice. Finally add your 2 tablespoon of soy sauce and you're ready to eat your meal.

# **Chicken curry**

Ingredients:

2 tbsp sunflower oil

1 onion, thinly sliced

2 garlic cloves, crushed

Thumb-sized piece of fresh ginger, grated

6 chicken thighs, boneless and skinless (or use veggies such as courgettes, beans, spinach as a vegetarian alternative)

3 tbsp medium spice paste (tikka works well)

400g can chopped tomatoes

100g full fat Greek yogurt

1 small bunch coriander, leaves chopped

50g ground almonds

naan breads or cooked basmati rice, to serve


Serves 4 people

Method:

1. Heat the oil in a large pan over a medium heat. Add the onion and a pinch of salt, and fry for 8-10 minutes, or until the onion has turned golden brown. Add the ginger and garlic and cook for a further minute.

2. Chop the chicken into chunky pieces, add to the pan, and fry for 5 minutes. Then add the spice paste and tomatoes along with 250ml of water. Bring to a boil, lower to a simmer and cook on a low heat for 25-30 minutes.

3. Add the yoghurt, coriander and ground almonds, season and serve with basmati rice and warm naan.

# Cheese and ham omelette

Ingredients:

50g of grated cheddar

2 slices of chopped ham

2 eggs

Milk

Salt and pepper

Method:

1. Break and mix the eggs, chopped ham and some of the cheese together in a bowl, and add a splash of milk plus a pinch of salt and pepper.

2. Heat a splash of olive oil in a small non-stick frying pan. Pour the mixture into the pan and cook for 4 minutes on a low heat until the underside is browned. Sprinkle over the remaining cheese, and place the pan under the grill for a further 2 mins until the cheese is bubbling and golden.

# **Bonus snack**

**Toasties:**

This may seem like a very easy meal to cook, and I hope that you already know how to make a toastie, but I can guarantee you that toasties are part of every student's staple diet. It is well worth investing £20 into a toastie maker at the start of the year, and this is made even cheaper if all of your flatmates chip in for it. Toasties are a brilliant last-minute meal to have before rushing off to a night out, and won't set you back much time at all.

For best results you want to butter both sides of the bread for the toastie. This causes both the outside and inside of the bread to have that golden crispy texture, making it that little bit nicer.

A very underrated sauce for our basic ham and cheese toasties is salad cream. It may sound like a strange combination, but after being introduced to it last year, all of my house were using it by the end.

# Household hacks

One of the things that most people take for granted before university is the household chores that your parents will often end up doing for you at home. It is very surprising how many freshers do not know how to use a washing machine, a tumble dryer, or even that you need to use washing-up liquid to wash dishes, so do not be like them!

This chapter will give you many different tips that can make your household chores much easier and quicker to do and make your flat feel more homely.

# The washing machine

This is a contraption that will cause even the brightest of student minds a world of trouble at some point during freshers. Whether it be shrinking all your clothes, turning all of your white's red, or losing half of your socks, washing can be a traumatic experience. This section will show you how to avoid these pitfalls that your fellow flatmates are bound to make.

### Shrinking problem:

This occurs when you wash certain clothes at too high a temperature. 40 degrees C is the safest option, and not much can go wrong.

If the washing machine was not hard enough, then the tumble dryer can also be a cause of clothes shrinking. Your clothes will have a label on them saying whether they are suitable for a tumble dryer, and it is very important that you check this before drying them. Clothes that are definitely not suitable for a dryer are woollen clothes and silk clothes, but other clothes may also not be suitable. I would recommend buying a small clothes horse for drying clothes (or a radiator rack), or you can just make a makeshift clothesline in your room instead using coat-hangers.

## Colours running:

Try to separate your clothes into the same colour groups. If this is not possible, then be sure to separate them into whites and colours. It is also more likely for colours to run in newer clothes, so be wary of this. Check the label to see if it says 'wash separately'. Washing clothes at a low temperature (e.g. 40 degrees C) helps to avoid colours running.

## Circuit laundry:

Most university halls have a system called circuit laundry, and it will be the bane of your life. It is a common laundry area, but instead of simply putting money into the washing machines, you have to deposit money onto the circuit app, select which machine you would like on the app, and pick what setting you would like your wash to be on. This also requires that you have wifi, or a phone signal in your washing area, which mine had neither of. There is also a minimum deposit of £10 for circuit, which means that most seniors (including myself) still have a wasted £5 or so on their circuit account. Be careful not to leave your clothes in the washing machine too long, because if left overnight they can start to smell worse than before you washed them.

# Cooking equipment

This next section will very much depend on what type of person you are. If you are a very clean person, and you always wash up your dishes after you have used them, then this section will not apply to you. However, from past experience, as the year goes on most students end up becoming far more relaxed when it comes to washing up after themselves (myself included). An easy way to minimise this problem, other than simply washing up after yourself, is to only bring two sets of everything meaning two plates, two sets of cutlery, two glasses etc. You can't be too messy if you don't have much mess to leave. If you have more than one friend coming round, then your fellow housemates are sure to be fine with you using some of their things!

Sometimes uni kitchens are not particularly big, and there isn't that much storage space. If everyone is bringing pots, pans, woks etc., then it can become a little crowded. It may be worth asking your flatmates if they want to share some of these items before going to uni, so that you will not all need to bring one of each item.

# Your room

University rooms can go one of two ways. You have got your messy rooms with clothes all over the floor and little decoration on the walls, and your clean rooms that are often very personalised and homely.

Messy rooms are for obvious reasons the worst of the two options, but unsurprisingly the most common of the two (especially for boys!). Messy rooms can lead to less productivity, less creativity, and can even contribute to depression. This is obviously what you want to avoid, and it really is not hard to do.

Why having a tidy room is better:

- You will be able to find everything much more easily and quickly.
- You will always know what clothes are clean, and what clothes are dirty.
- It will lift your mood and you will be more willing to work in you room.
- You will be more social because you won't be embarrassed about inviting people into your room.
- Studies have shown that a tidy room helps you to sleep better and lessens stress.

Personalizing your room is another great stress reliever. Putting pictures of your friends and family on your wall will help with any home sickness that you are feeling and remind you to keep regular contact with all of them. Posters and LED lighting will also boost your mood and increase productivity.

# **Towels and bedsheets**

You may or may not be aware of this, but towels and bedsheets need regular washing! It is far too common that freshers either only bring one towel, or one set of bedsheets, and after two weeks end up smelling worse after a shower than they did before.

Bed sheets (including pillowcase, and duvet cover) should be washed at a minimum every two weeks! There are far too many freshers who you will ask at Christmas time how often they wash their sheets, and they will reply 'huh, you have to wash bed sheets?' Each night your body sheds about 15 million skin cells, which build up if you do not wash your sheets regularly. You are essentially providing food for thousands of dust mites, which about 5% of people are allergic to. Many bacteria and fungi can also build up if your sheets are left unwashed for long enough, with studies finding that after one month bedsheets can have more bacteria than toilet seats.

Towels also need to be washed regularly. Towels should be washed approximately after every four uses and should be allowed to dry properly every time before being used. Just as with bed sheets, towels will end up carrying millions of germs after only a few uses, so be sure to stay on top of washing them.

# **Halls vs houses**

If your halls of residence are not quite as nice as you were hoping they would be, then don't worry it will get better. It is fairly common for first year halls to just have a kitchen table, and not to have any sofas or a TV. However, in my opinion, this is all part of the fresher experience that you will grow to enjoy. When you move into your second and third years, you are very likely to move into a shared house that nearly always has a nice living room area with sofas, and usually even has a garden as well. Your rooms will also be much bigger in your house, but don't be surprised if you end up missing your little halls rooms after you have moved out.

# Money hacks

Unless you are very fortunate, it is true that being a student and having lots of money don't go hand in hand. 70% of students get overdrawn during their first year of uni, so don't be alarmed if this happens to you. It is likely that most of your flatmates and friends are just as tight for money as you are. There are, however, many little things that you can do that will save you lots of money over the course of the year, and help you stay out of that dreaded overdraft.

# Shop at LIDL or ALDI

You will be very surprised how much money you can save if you simply shop at one of the discount supermarkets such as LIDL or ALDI. You may be wary to move on from the major supermarkets that you may be used to at home, but there really isn't much difference in quality. Compared with Tesco's, Sainbury's or Asda, LIDL is by far the cheaper option.

During my first year of university, I spent an average of £30 pounds per week on food when shopping at Tesco's (which was located very close to my student flat). Then in my second year I switched to LIDL, and my weekly food shop fell to approximately £25 per week. Most students are at uni for between 30-40 weeks of the year, so this could save you up to £200 per year!

# Reduced section

If you are extra strapped for cash, then you can also look at the reduced section in Tesco's (or other supermarkets). You will often be able to find sandwiches and snacks for as little as about 20p, so it is a real money saver. Buying meat in the reduced section can also be a great way to find bargains.

Don't be alarmed if the sell by date is a day or two away, as you can simply freeze it, and it will still be good to eat for a few weeks after.

# **Packed lunch**

Bringing a packed lunch with you to lectures or the library is also a very good and easy way to save some money. You may think that £3 for a meal deal isn't very expensive, but when you do that every day it does add up. Making yourself a packed lunch also means that you will eat healthier foods and that you can also pick exactly what you want in your sandwiches with more variety.

# Pre-drink well

Drinks in clubs are often sold at an extortionate price. A single shot in a club (which would cost you approximately 50p if you bought the spirit from a shop) will often cost in the vicinity of £3! Spending too much on drinks in clubs is the number one reason why 70% of students end up in overdraft. It is always best to pre-drink well, so that you're ready to start dancing when you get to the club. Not only does this save you money, but it also saves the time of having to queue for drinks at the bar.

If you are planning on drinking in pubs and clubs, then look for student nights and happy hours. Clubs and pubs will often serve 2 for 1 cocktails or £1 shots before 11pm, or clubs will have student nights where all drinks are cheaper than usual. Going for rounds with friends in clubs is time saving, but often ends up with one or two people buying more drinks than the rest, so be wary of this.

# Money saving apps and cards

**NUS card** – This stands for the National Union of Students and it only costs £13. It gets you discounts at over 250 shops, so will pay itself back within a matter of weeks.

**Squirrel (app)** – This app lets you separate the money that you have for savings, spending and bills so you can see exactly how much you've got left each month. Squirrel can also look after your money and deliver it to you in monthly or weekly instalments.

**Splitwise (app)** - Ordered pizzas for a flat movie marathon? Planning a flat day out? Splitwise removes all the hassle of asking people to chip in. Just create a group or an event and everybody can see exactly what they owe and who they need to pay.

**TopCashback** - More than 4,500 retailers work with TopCashback, to give you some money back from your spending. Get money back from online shopping, and upload photos of physical receipts of in-store purchases. After a while, you'll build up a pot of cash in your TopCashback account, which can then be withdrawn at any time.

Your university will give you the whole Microsoft Office package, so this means that you won't need to buy any of these products before. This is a great money saver.

# Getting a part time job

Sometimes these little money saving tips aren't quite enough, and you find yourself a little too far into your overdraft for your own liking. Many students end up getting part time jobs whilst studying at uni, in order to earn a bit of extra cash, but is it worth it?

Positives of getting a part time job:

- You get more money.
- Good chance to meet new people.
- Gives you more structure.
- Gives you work experience which can also be good for your CV.
- Means you don't have to worry about cash as much and can enjoy yourself a little more.


Negatives of getting a part time job:

- Less time for studying and learning.
- You have lectures during the day, so student jobs tend to be in the evening or nights such as pubs and clubs. This means that you may not be able to go out partying when the rest of your friends are and may not get as much sleep as you need.
- Can be stressful.

61

- Can prevent you from going home if you live far away, because asking for time off work can be tough.

Overall, it depends very much on the person whether it is worth getting a part time job or not. Generally, people that do work at university tend to get jobs in their later years when the social side becomes slightly less important, but it is very much up to you.

# Lecture tips

This book may have had a large emphasis on the social aspect of university, but hey, you are a fresher. That is what the first year of uni is all about. However, lectures and doing well in your degree are still very important and this is the reason why you have gone to university after all. It is very possible to stay up to date on your lectures and coursework, whilst still experiencing all the social side that university has to offer!

For most subjects you will find that the level of work is similar to that of your second year of A Level, and will be a very important base for moving to the more advanced content in later years to come.

The amount of lecture and tutorial hours that you will have vary from course to course, but do not be alarmed, for most courses it is far less than you would have had at school. Most subjects such as Business, Languages, Geography… have approximately 9 hours of lectures, and 1-2 hours of tutorials, and maybe 1 hour of seminars each week. There is a slight jump up for those who study anything medicine or law related, and other subjects that involve practicals such as Engineering, which tend to have between 18-25 contact hours per week.

# The 9am myth

You may already be dreading the prospect of waking up for 9am lectures (especially if you are unlucky enough to have one on a Thursday morning), but they are not quite as bad as they seem. All lectures actually start five minutes past the hour, so every 9am actually starts at 9:05. This gives you an extra five minutes in bed, which may not seem like much, but you will be sure to be grateful for at the time.

# Recorded lectures

Almost all your lecturers will record their lectures and post them onto your university online platform. This allows you to re-watch any lectures that were particularly difficult and is an absolute life-saver when it comes to exam time. It also means that if you do happen to miss that Thursday 9am lecture, then it is not too bad as you can simply watch it online later. Be careful though, skipping lectures and saying to yourself that you will just watch them later can be a slippery slope to get very behind on your content.

# **<u>Note taking</u>**

There are many ways that people revise and take notes for lectures, and you must figure out what works best for you. The way I take notes now is very different to what many other people in my lectures do.

Before uni I did not really know what my preferred way to take notes was, so I've trialled a few different methods. In first year, I used to just take notes in a notebook, but there are a few problems with this. Lecturers talk quite fast, so it is difficult to keep up and listen to what they are saying at the same time. I then started bringing my laptop with me instead but encountered the same problems. I also found that if I was frantically writing all the time, then despite getting the content written down I actually didn't take any of it in.

I had a few lecturers who would print out the lecture slides as a handout with a few words missing, which

I found to be a far better note taking method. It keeps you engaged, and lets you follow the fast-paced lectures. Sadly, not many lecturers are willing to do this so don't rely on this method of note taking. However, most lecturers will make their lecture slides available online before the lecture, so you could download them to your laptop and make notes on the slides in the same way during the lecture.

Ultimately, I've found that the method that works for me is to simply not make any notes during the lecture, and just listen and make sure I actually understand what the lecturer is talking about. Then if it is a tough lecture I will go back and make notes on the recording of the lecture, which you are able to pause and un-pause so that you do not get left behind. It is also important to do further reading about the topics that your lecturers are talking about, as often the lecture content itself won't quite be enough detail that would be needed for your essays or exams.

# Tutorials, Lectures and Seminars: what's the difference?

You are very likely to see all three of these on your timetable in freshers' week and you may be a little confused as to what the difference between them is.

Lectures – these are the most common of the three and are where you will be taught all your course content. They take place in big lecture halls (depending on the size of your course) and can have up to 250 people in them! Do not be alarmed though, audience participation is usually not mandatory in lectures although your lecturer will still ask some questions if you are feeling confident.

Tutorials – These are much smaller than lectures (rarely have more than 15 people). They are an opportunity for you to discuss the content from the lectures in more detail and ask the lecturer any questions you may have. Tutorials are definitely the most important of the three, because they allow you to understand the hardest content in the lectures, and tutorial questions often come up in exam papers.

Seminars – These are combinations of both the lectures and tutorials and are usually slightly larger groups than tutorials (usually around 20 people). Usually there will be a set theme or topic to discuss in a seminar and the lecturer may ask you to answer questions. If you have a presentation to do, then this will usually be done in a seminar.

# **Library**

This is a dreaded place for many students, and you may think that you won't be using the library very much, but trust me, when it is exam time, you will be sure to be spending most of your days in your library. Almost every student will have to experience a 4am library session the day before an exam (my record is 6am before a 9am exam, not advisable), but luckily this is much more likely to be in your second and third years of uni.

I have always found that it is far easier to work in the library than it is to work in your room back home. It is nice to separate your work place and your relaxation place, so that when you get home you don't even need to think about doing work. There is usually a silent section, and a chattier section of the library, so you can sit in either according to how much you would like to concentrate on your work, and if you are there on your own or with friends.

I have always found myself being far more productive when I go to the library with course mates, because we can go through the work together, and help each other out. You are also very likely to have group coursework to do, and the library is a very good place to prepare for this.

It is also a good place to look up readings and journals, and will also have a few printers and photocopiers that you can use. You simply have to put a few pounds on your student card to pay for them.

# **Final words**

University for me and many of my friends has been some of best years of our lives (especially being a fresher!) It teaches you independence, social skills, organization, and much more. You will make lifelong friends, and many memories that will last forever.

There are bound to be times when university throws adversity and hurdles towards you, but if you can manage to follow even some of these tips and tricks, it is sure to make your university life much easier, and more enjoyable! I know that if I had known these tips before uni, I would have settled in more quickly, and saved myself a lot of money along the way.

Printed in Great Britain
by Amazon